NFL TODAY

THE STORY OF THE
TAMPA BAY BUCCANEERS

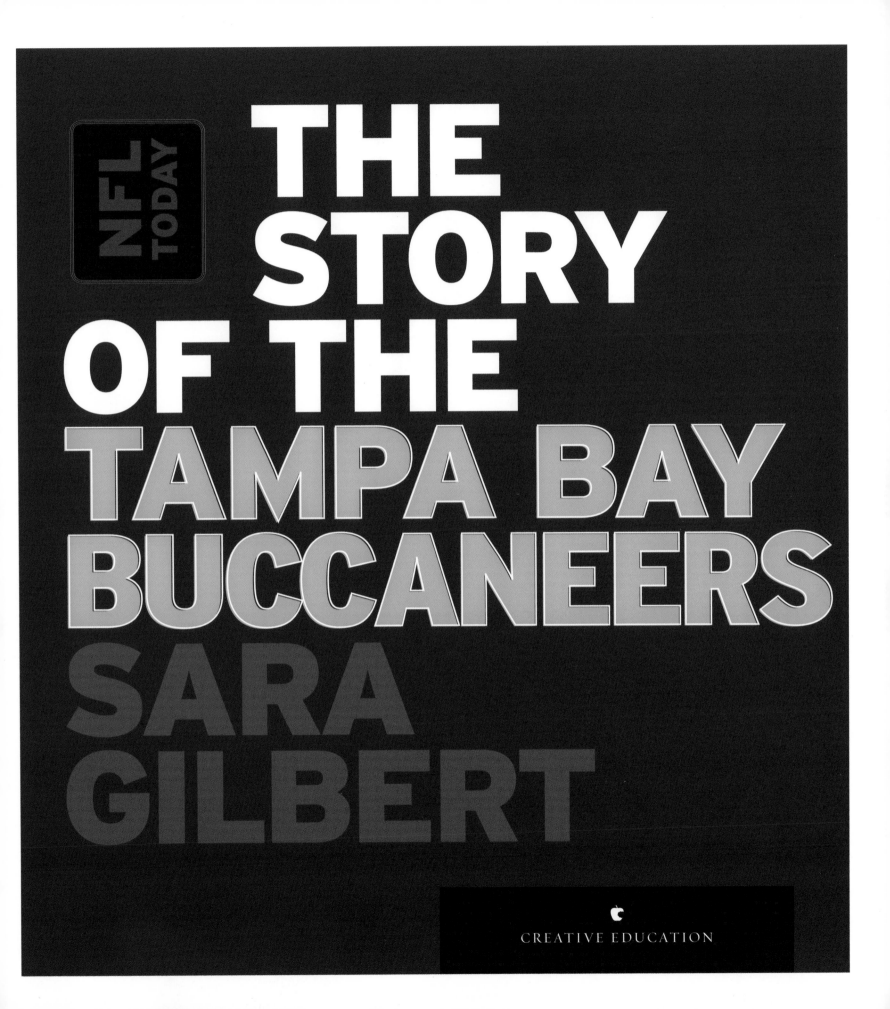

NFL TODAY

THE STORY OF THE TAMPA BAY BUCCANEERS

SARA GILBERT

CREATIVE EDUCATION

Cover: Running back Gary Anderson (top), wide
receiver Michael Clayton (bottom)
Page 2: Wide receiver Maurice Stovall
Pages 4–5: 2002 Tampa Bay Buccaneers
Pages 6–7: Buccaneers offense, 2004

....

Published by Creative Education
P.O. Box 227, Mankato, Minnesota 56002
Creative Education is an imprint of
The Creative Company
www.thecreativecompany.us

Design and production by Blue Design
Design Associate: Sarah Yakawonis
Printed in the United States of America

Photographs by Alamy (Andre Jenny, JTB Photo
Communications,Inc.), Getty Images (Al Bello,
Markus Boesch/Allsport, Scott Cunningham, James
Drake/Sports Illustrated, Jonathan Ferrey, Andy
Hayt, Wesley Hitt, Jed Jacobsohn, Andy Lyons/
Allsport, Al Messerschmidt, Al Messerschmidt/NFL,
Ronald C. Modra/Sports Imagery, Michael Montes/
NFL, Peter Muhly/AFP, Peter Newcomb/AFP, NFL
Photos, Lynn Pelham//Time & Life Pictures, Doug
Pensinger, Joe Robbins, Scott Rovak/AFP, Jerry
Wachter/Sports Illustrated)

Library of Congress Cataloging-in-Publication Data

Gilbert, Sara.
The story of the Tampa Bay Buccaneers / Sara
Gilbert.
p. cm. — (NFL today)
Includes index.
ISBN 978-1-58341-772-0
1. Tampa Bay Buccaneers (Football team)—History—
Juvenile literature. I. Title. II. Series.

GV956.T35G55 2009
796.332'640975965—dc22   2008022705

First Edition
9 8 7 6 5 4 3 2 1

BUCS WIN!

THE ROAD TO THE CHAMPIONSHIP

For the Tampa Bay Buccaneers, this indeed is a Super Sunday.

The Bucs, who never before this season had advanced to the NFL's championship game, beat the Oakland Raiders tonight at Qualcomm Stadium in Super Bowl XXXVII in a game that will be remembered for a long time after Tampa Bay fans...

...in the same way a franchise that went to the non-winningest...

fore winning the next-to-last game of the 1977 season. And, though Tampa Bay had advanced to the NFC Championship Game twice before in 1979 and 1999, the team's history had been more a tale of woe than success.

But in his first year after coming over from the Raiders in a controversial deal, coach Jon Gruden took the team to the Super Bowl...

CONTENTS

SETTING SAIL 8

FROM BAD TO WORSE 18

DUNGY'S DEFENSE 24

PUTTING THE PIECES TOGETHER 38

INDEX 48

ON THE SIDELINES

CELEBRATING THE STREAK'S END 12

FASHION STATEMENTS 20

DRAFT DAY DISAPPOINTMENTS 27

SHIPSHAPE STADIUM 31

COURTING A COACH 41

RUNNING FOR THE RECORD 42

MEET THE BUCCANEERS

LEE ROY SELMON 11

DOUG WILLIAMS 15

DERRICK BROOKS 23

MIKE ALSTOTT 28

WARREN SAPP 34

TONY DUNGY 46

SETTING SAIL

X - - - - - - - - - - - -

The city of Tampa started as a small American Indian village next to a bay on the west coast of Florida. Spanish explorers found it during their search for gold in the early 1500s. Although those explorers were persuaded to continue their quest farther north, legend has it that a Spanish pirate captain named José Gaspar was not as easily discouraged. Gaspar and his crew roamed the southwestern coast of Florida, seeking jewels and riches, for years.

T oday, Tampa honors that legend with the annual Gasparilla Pirate Festival, which draws more than 400,000 people to a city that is home to about 330,000 residents. Although the area is also known for its beautiful, white-sand beaches and subtropical climate, there is an enduring fascination with the region's swashbuckling history. That helps explain why, when the National Football League (NFL) granted an expansion team to the area to begin play in 1976, area residents voted to name it the Buccaneers.

When longtime University of Southern California coach John McKay was hired to lead the expansion Tampa Bay Buccaneers, he urged fans to be patient. It would take five years, he said, to turn the new franchise's collection of aging veterans and inexperienced rookies into a playoff-caliber team.

X The Gasparilla Pirate Festival, which has been held in Tampa Bay for more than a century, takes place annually in late January—generally just before the NFL's Super Bowl.

But even McKay, who was known for his easygoing style and quick wit, ran short of patience during the Buccaneers' first two seasons. In 1976, with veteran quarterback Steve Spurrier leading the offense, Tampa Bay lost all 14 of its games. Kicker Dave Green scored the team's first points, a 39-yard field goal in a 14–9 loss to the Buffalo Bills, but in five games that season, the Bucs couldn't manage to score a single point. McKay tried to make light of it. "It is at times like this that we thank our stars that we do have a sense of humor," he said.

But when the losing streak continued deep into the following season, McKay wasn't laughing. Neither was defensive end Lee Roy Selmon, the team's first-round pick in the 1976 NFL Draft, who had won the team's Rookie of the Year award during Tampa Bay's winless season. Selmon led a defensive line that included ends Council Rudolph and Dave Pear. Tampa Bay's defense was ultimately responsible for introducing the Bucs to the win column on December 11, 1977, when it intercepted six passes and returned an NFL-record three of them for touchdowns. After having lost 26 consecutive games and set a dubious NFL record in the process, the Buccaneers finally notched their first win, 33–14, over the New Orleans Saints.

LEE ROY SELMON

DEFENSIVE END
BUCCANEERS SEASONS: 1976-84
HEIGHT: 6-FOOT-3
WEIGHT: 256 POUNDS

Tampa Bay couldn't afford to waste its first-ever draft choice in 1976. So the new team selected the best player available: Lee Roy Selmon, a huge but humble defensive end from the University of Oklahoma. Selmon earned team Rookie of the Year honors in 1976 and quickly endeared himself to fans and teammates. Although he was known as a genuinely nice guy who helped players up after knocking them down, opponents knew to respect his skills on the field. David Whitehurst, a quarterback with the Green Bay Packers who played against Selmon, called him "the best defensive lineman I've ever seen. He'd make the play, turn around, and line up again. That's how the game is meant to be played." Selmon spent nine years in Tampa and likely would have played longer if a back injury hadn't forced his retirement in 1984. His jersey number, 63, was retired by the Bucs in 1986, and he was inducted into the Pro Football Hall of Fame in 1995. A chain of restaurants in Florida that serves his mother's recipes for chili, meatloaf, and strawberry compote now bears his name.

CELEBRATING THE STREAK'S END

The Tampa Bay Buccaneers started celebrating their first win—a 33–14 victory over the New Orleans Saints in December 1977—on the plane ride home to Florida. The players smoked cigars, and coach John McKay (pictured) made the rounds to shake everyone's hand. But the real celebration began when the plane landed in Tampa and the players found more than 8,000 fans waiting for them at team headquarters, One Buccaneer Place. The streets were too crowded to drive through, so McKay climbed atop a parked car to give a brief speech to the crowd. Fans who had spent 26 games waiting for a win, and who had often chanted "Throw McKay in the Bay" during the losing streak, were now cheering for him. Someone even waved a homemade sign that read, "Retrieve McKay from the Bay!" As the Buccaneer Band played their own version of "When the Saints Go Marching In," changing the refrain to "Oh when the Saints go falling down …," McKay summed up the day's events in one sentence: "It was the greatest victory in the history of the world."

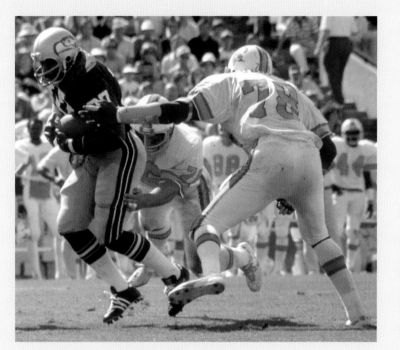

The Bucs defeated the St. Louis Cardinals at Tampa Stadium the following week and ended the season at 2–12, in last place in the National Football Conference (NFC) Central Division. Still, it was something to build on. And with a new quarterback—the long and lanky Doug Williams, who had been selected in the first round of the 1978 NFL Draft—Tampa Bay seemed poised to climb out of the cellar in its third season. The team had a respectable 4–6 record when Williams's jaw was broken in a game against the Los Angeles Rams. The Bucs won only one more game the rest of the season.

Williams was back in 1979 and better than ever. So was running back Ricky Bell, who rushed for more than 1,000 yards. Tampa Bay won its first five games and eked out a 3–0 victory over the Kansas City Chiefs in the last week of

the season to earn both the NFC Central championship and a playoff berth. Just three years after going 0–14, Tampa Bay had achieved a 10–6 record. Jubilant Bucs fans held up banners that read, "From Worst to First."

In the playoffs, Tampa Bay defeated the Philadelphia Eagles 24–17 to reach the NFC Championship Game against the Rams. A victory meant a berth in the Super Bowl. The Buccaneers held their own in a tough defensive battle against the Rams but came up short, 9–0. "My gosh, we could taste it," said Bucs linebacker Richard Wood. "The Super Bowl. It was right there for us. But you know what? You're not promised anything in this game."

The Buccaneers were not even promised a winning season the following year. In fact, 1980 ended with a disappointing 5–10–1 record, putting Tampa Bay back near the bottom of the standings. But in 1981, with running back James Wilder adding flash to the offense, the Bucs bounced back with a 9–7 record and another division title. This time, however, the Dallas Cowboys drubbed Tampa Bay in the opening round of the playoffs, 38–0.

A players' strike shortened the 1982 season to just 9 games, but the 5–4 Buccaneers were one of 16 teams selected to play in an expanded Super Bowl tournament. As luck would

DOUG WILLIAMS

QUARTERBACK
BUCCANEERS SEASONS: 1978-82
HEIGHT: 6-FOOT-4
WEIGHT: 220 POUNDS

Although he was not the first African American quarterback to play in the NFL, Doug Williams was among the

most successful. He was drafted by the Buccaneers with the 17th overall pick in the 1978 NFL Draft and soon

made an impact on the hapless team. With Williams under center, the Buccaneers found their way to the

playoffs for the first time—and for the second and third times as well. He threw a career-high 20 touchdown

passes in 1980 and tallied a total of 73 in his time with the team. Unfortunately, when Williams asked for a

raise after leading Tampa Bay to the playoffs in 1982, team ownership countered with a figure that Williams

considered unfair. Instead of negotiating, Williams decided to leave the team—angrily. He went on to play two

seasons in the rival United States Football League before returning to the NFL and becoming the Most Valuable

Player (MVP) of Super Bowl XXII with the Washington Redskins in 1987. After coaching at the college level for

several years, Williams returned to Tampa Bay in 2004 and has been the team's personnel executive since then.

X Halfback Ricky Bell was selected with the first overall pick of the 1977 NFL Draft, but heart disease shortened his career and his life; he played just 6 seasons and died at age 29.

have it, they drew the Cowboys again in the first round and were again defeated, 30–17.

That's when things started unraveling in Tampa Bay. In the off-season, Williams entered into a bitter contract dispute with team owner Hugh Culverhouse that ended the quarterback's tenure with the team. After an embarrassing 2–14 season in 1983 and a career-ending back injury to Selmon in 1984, Coach McKay gave notice as well. His replacement, Leeman Bennett, confidently told fans, "I expect our team to contend for the NFC Central Division title now, not later."

James Wilder became known as a workhorse running back in Tampa Bay; in 1984, he toted the ball a league-high 407 times, scoring 13 touchdowns.

FROM BAD
TO WORSE

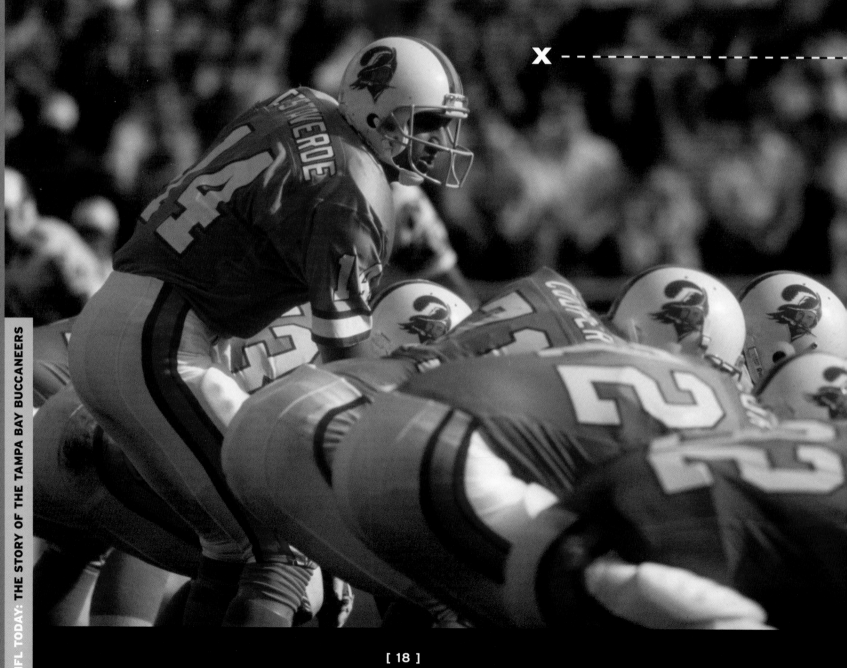

Bennett's Bucs had a hard time living up to his expectations. The 1985 season started with nine losses and ended with just two wins. The only bright side was that, as owners of the worst record in the league, Tampa Bay secured the first overall pick in the 1986 NFL Draft. But even that turned disastrous. The team selected Bo Jackson, a fast and powerful running back who had won the Heisman Trophy as college football's best player in 1985. Given the option of signing with the struggling Buccaneers or playing professional baseball, the versatile Jackson chose baseball.

By the end of 1986, the Buccaneers had given up on Bennett, whose two-year record with the team stood at an abysmal 4–28. They had also given up on quarterback Steve Young, who had been sacked 68 times in 2 seasons. He was traded to the San Francisco 49ers (where he would become a star) to clear the way for young quarterback Vinny Testaverde. Sure that Testaverde was exactly what they needed, the Buccaneers signed him to a 6-year contract worth $8.2 million, making him the richest rookie in the NFL.

New coach Ray Perkins put a lot of faith in Testaverde's arm and in rookie wide receiver Mark Carrier's sure hands. And to make sure his team would be in great physical shape, Perkins started training camp with three grueling workouts

X Although he would later earn Pro Bowl honors with two different NFL teams, Vinny Testaverde struggled in his six Bucs seasons, throwing more interceptions than touchdowns every year.

FASHION STATEMENTS

It wasn't just the Buccaneers' record that was bad during the early years of Tampa Bay's history. The players wore uniforms that were the epitome of 1970s fashion trends. The combination of bright orange jerseys, white pants, and high orange socks became jokingly known as "creamsicles," after the ice cream treat. The Bucs' white helmets were decorated with red and orange stripes, as well as with the image of "Bucco Bruce," an orange pirate wearing a feathered hat and biting on a knife. Remarkably, the Tampa fans proudly wore bold orange outfits to the games. So impressive was the combined effect that when the Philadelphia Eagles came to town for the 1979 playoffs, the Eagles players couldn't help but notice the sea of orange in the stands. "That crowd was the [darndest] thing," laughed Philadelphia linebacker Claude Humphrey. In 1997, the team introduced a new, less-orange look: pewter pants and white jerseys, with orange only outlining dark red numbers. The team unveiled a more swashbuckling logo as well: a skull and two crossed swords on a blood-red pirate flag.

each day. Although that approach appeared to be working when the team routed the Atlanta Falcons 48–10 in the season opener, the players were too tired to keep it up. The Buccaneers finished 4–11 in the strike-shortened 1987 season, then 5–11 in both 1988 and 1989. Before the end of the 1990 season, Perkins was fired.

Tampa Bay's next coach, Richard Williamson, lasted only one season, an embarrassing 3–13 campaign. Former Cincinnati Bengals coach Sam Wyche took the reins in 1992, inheriting a Buccaneers squad that hadn't posted a winning season in 10 years. Unfortunately, even Wyche, who had taken the Bengals to the Super Bowl in 1988, wasn't able to stop that streak in his four seasons with the team.

Part of the team's problem was at the quarterback position. Testaverde had been a disappointment, throwing more interceptions than touchdowns before being released at the end of 1992. But his teammates knew he wasn't the only player to blame. "Everybody wants to say it's Vinny's fault," said linebacker Broderick Thomas. "We've got a young team. He's a young quarterback. He's been taking the rips and hard knocks since he's been here. It ain't his fault."

The closest the Buccaneers came to a winning record under Coach Wyche was a 6–10 season in 1994, when rookie

running back Errict Rhett's 192-yard rushing effort against the Washington Redskins was the highlight of a four-game winning streak. But new quarterback Trent Dilfer struggled even more than Testaverde had, throwing 18 interceptions and only 4 touchdown passes in 1995. It was no surprise when Wyche was fired after a 7–9 finish in 1995. "This team is far better than it was four years ago," Wyche said as he left. "A good man will come in here and reap some of the benefits of the hard work we put in."

Than good man was Tony Dungy, a longtime assistant coach who had earned a reputation as a defensive mastermind with the Minnesota Vikings. When he took over as head coach in 1996, Dungy inherited a trio of young defensive players—tackle Warren Sapp, linebacker Derrick Brooks, and strong safety John Lynch—who would prove pivotal in reversing the team's fortunes. But Dungy was also cursed with a lifeless offense that generated only 21 touchdowns in 16 games in 1996. That season marked Tampa Bay's 14th consecutive losing effort. Neither Dungy nor the young players in white and orange were willing to extend that streak another year.

DERRICK BROOKS

LINEBACKER
BUCCANEERS SEASONS: 1995-2008
HEIGHT: 6 FEET
WEIGHT: 235 POUNDS

By the time he graduated from high school in 1991, Derrick Brooks was already a big-time football star. The young linebacker had led his high school team to a state championship and was regarded as one of the best high school football players in Florida's history. But that was only the beginning. Brooks, a first-round draft pick in 1995, became one of the premier linebackers in the NFL. A prolific tackler who was light enough on his feet to return the occasional interception for a touchdown, Brooks went to the Pro Bowl 10 straight times—becoming one of only 4 players in NFL history to do so. But he was respected as much for his work off the field as on it. Brooks was well known for his charity work, especially his advocacy for the importance of education. He founded the Brooks' Bunch organization to provide scholarships to youth in the Tampa Bay area and helped start a new high school. In 2003, Florida governor Jeb Bush named him to the Board of Trustees of Florida State University, where Brooks had played college ball.

DUNGY'S DEFENSE

Something seemed different about the 1997 Buccaneers—and it was more than just the sleek new pewter and red uniforms that the players were wearing. After more than a decade of slow starts and sad finishes, Tampa Bay won its first five games. The unlikely hero was former scapegoat Trent Dilfer, whose newfound patience was paying off in the form of more touchdown passes and fewer interceptions. With fullback Mike Alstott bulldozing his way into the end zone and elusive running back Warrick Dunn scampering for nearly 1,000 yards, Tampa Bay's offense was improving.

ut it was the defense—led by Sapp, Brooks, Lynch, and linebacker Hardy Nickerson—that stole the show. Tampa Bay's "D" was among the NFL's best in 1997, setting a team record with 44 quarterback sacks. After crushing the Chicago Bears 31–15 in the final game of the regular season, the 10–6 Buccaneers sailed into the postseason.

It seemed fitting that the last game ever played in Houlihan's Stadium, as Tampa Stadium had been renamed,

X Halfback Warrick Dunn weighed just 180 pounds—a featherweight by NFL standards—but beat many a defender with his surprising strength and ability to instantly change direction.

DRAFT DAY DISAPPOINTMENTS

The Buccaneers' first-ever draft choice may have been their best: defensive end Lee Roy Selmon (pictured, number 63), the team's first (and, as of 2008, only) representative in the Pro Football Hall of Fame. Not every selection worked out as well. The Bucs passed over Tony Dorsett, a Hall of Fame running back, in favor of running back Ricky Bell in the 1977 NFL Draft. They used the first overall pick in 1987 on quarterback Vinny Testaverde, who had only a mediocre career in Tampa Bay, while the man he replaced—eventual Hall-of-Famer Steve Young—won three Super Bowl titles with the San Francisco 49ers. The biggest draft debacle, however, may have been using the first overall pick in 1986 to take running back Bo Jackson, even though Jackson had announced that he did not want to sign with the last-place team. Despite a reported 5-year, $7-million contract offer from the Bucs, Jackson opted to play professional baseball with the Kansas City Royals instead. He signed with the Oakland Raiders football team in 1987 and played there for four seasons.

MIKE ALSTOTT

FULLBACK
BUCCANEERS SEASONS: 1996-2006
HEIGHT: 6-FOOT-1
WEIGHT: 248 POUNDS

There's a reason why Mike "The A-Train" Alstott was so good at running over defensive backs and breaking free of tacklers who were trying to bring him down. Part of his training routine during his college career at Purdue University involved pulling a Jeep through the campus parking lot, then pushing it back. After a workout like that, even the largest defenders weren't much of an obstacle for Alstott. Over the course of his 12 seasons with the team, he set a franchise record for touchdowns scored, with 71. Alstott also had the honor of scoring the Buccaneers' first-ever Super Bowl touchdown on a 15-yard run. For his efforts, Alstott was sent to the Pro Bowl six times and was pictured on the cover of the *NFL Xtreme* video game for PlayStation in 1998. Although Alstott contemplated retirement after both the 2005 and 2006 seasons, it wasn't until a neck injury sidelined him in 2007 that he tearfully announced his retirement from football. "Though mentally I feel like I can continue, physically I can't," he said. "It's been a great ride, an unbelievable ride."

was the team's first playoff game in 15 years. And it was

a fond farewell, as 73,361 fans showed up to watch the

Buccaneers make easy work of the Detroit Lions in the first-

round matchup. But then it was on to the frozen tundra of

Green Bay's Lambeau Field, where the Super Bowl-bound

Packers ended the Buccaneers' season with a 21–7 rout.

The Bucs hoped to build on that success when they moved

into the brand-new Raymond James Stadium in 1998. And

although they won their first game there, the team sputtered

through the first half of the season. Even after winning four

of its last five games to finish at 8–8, Tampa Bay sat in third

X Built at a cost of $169 million, Raymond James Stadium played host to Super Bowl XXXV just three years after it opened in 1998.

place in the NFC Central and out of the playoffs.

The main problem in 1998 was a mediocre offense. Dilfer was just average, with 21 touchdown passes and 15 interceptions, and kicker Michael Husted missed seven key field goals during the season. To add depth at those positions, the Buccaneers selected quarterback Shaun King and kicker Martin Gramatica in the 1999 NFL Draft. King took over for Dilfer halfway through the 1999 season and sparked a six-game winning streak, while Gramatica kicked 106 total points as a rookie. Despite a 3–4 start, Tampa Bay rebounded to set a franchise record with an 11–5 finish.

The Bucs entered the postseason optimistically. But in the third quarter of the first playoff game against the Redskins, they were down 13–0. Then Lynch made a sensational interception at the Tampa Bay 27-yard line. He ran to the sidelines, where his offensive teammates were standing, spiked the ball, and yelled, "Do something!" Two plays later, Alstott ran the ball into the end zone to make it 13–7. After the Tampa Bay defense recovered a fumble, King tossed a touchdown pass to tight end John Davis, giving Tampa Bay a 14–13 victory.

The following week, the Bucs faced the St. Louis Rams in the NFC Championship Game. Although Tampa Bay's stingy

SHIPSHAPE STADIUM

For the first two decades of the Tampa Bay Buccaneers' history, the team played at Tampa Stadium, also known as "The Big Sombrero" because its shape resembled the traditional round Mexican hat. The Big Sombrero hosted two Super Bowls and was home to the Buccaneers until 1998, when the team moved to the brand-new Raymond James Stadium. The Buccaneers share the stadium with a local college football team and other annual events, but there's no question who the building was designed for. Just below the upper deck sits a 103-foot-long, 43-ton steel and concrete pirate ship. With an enormous skull mounted on the front and with cannons on the deck that are loaded to launch T-shirts and confetti when the Bucs score, the ship has become one of the defining images of the team. The lively music played during games adds to the atmosphere; when the song "Yo Ho (A Pirate's Life for Me)" blares out of the public address system, T-shirts, beads, and other prizes are thrown off the ship to the fans below.

X A native of Argentina, Martin Gramatica boasted one of the strongest kicking legs in football, connecting on 5 field goals of 50 yards or longer in both 2000 and 2002.

defense limited the normally high-powered Rams to just five points until late in the fourth quarter, St. Louis scored a touchdown with just two minutes left to win 11–6. For the second time in franchise history, the Bucs had just missed the Super Bowl.

Coach Dungy knew he had a championship-caliber defense. What he needed was a more productive offense. So, in 2000, the team traded for flamboyant wide receiver Keyshawn Johnson, whose eight touchdown receptions helped lead the Bucs to a 10–6 record and back to the playoffs. In 2001,

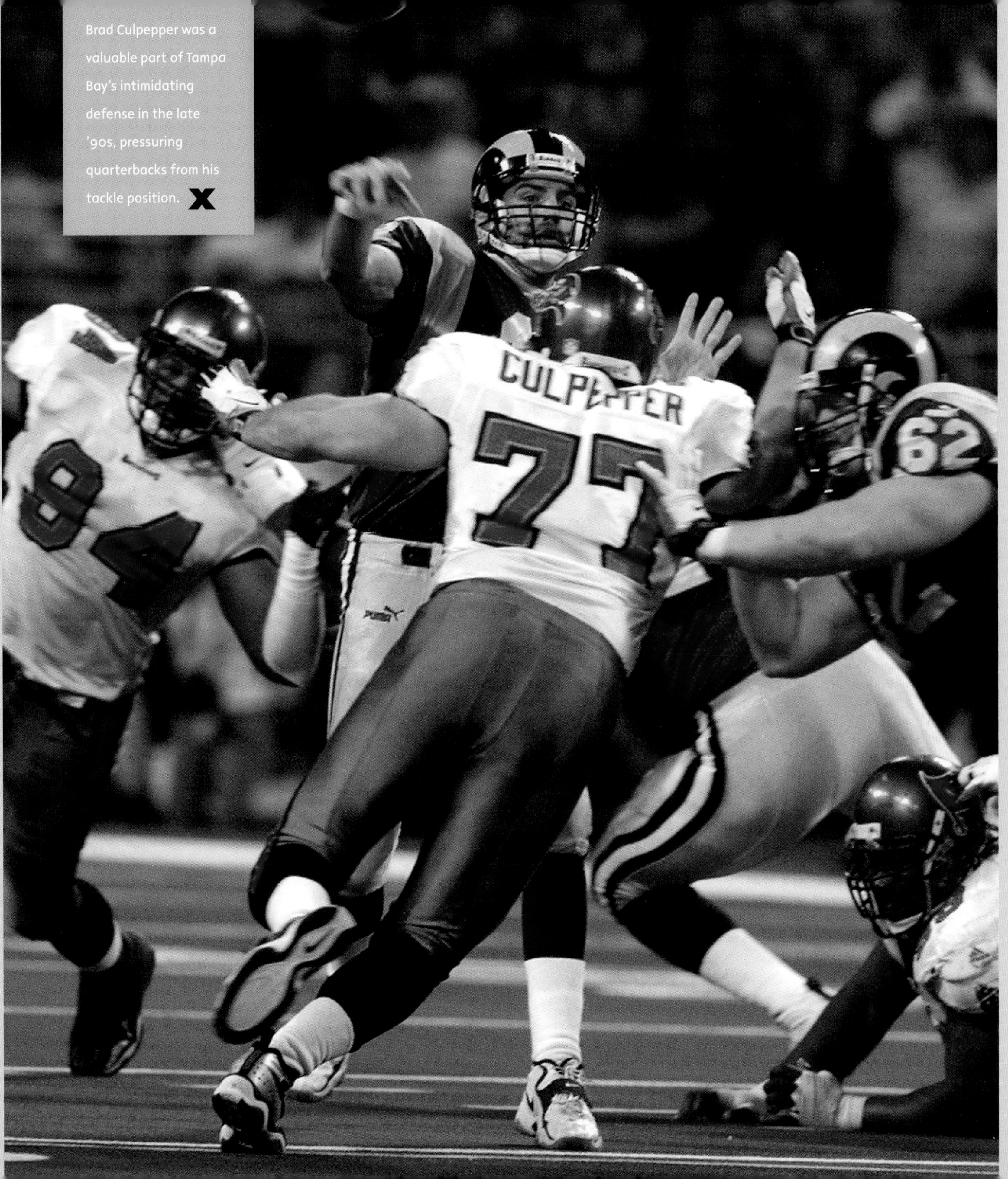

Brad Culpepper was a valuable part of Tampa Bay's intimidating defense in the late '90s, pressuring quarterbacks from his tackle position.

WARREN SAPP

DEFENSIVE TACKLE
BUCCANEERS SEASONS: 1995-2003
HEIGHT: 6-FOOT-2
WEIGHT: 303 POUNDS

It was hard to not notice Warren Sapp. Not only did the hulking defensive tackle have an intimidating physical presence, but he also had a penchant for making outrageous comments both on and off the field. When he wasn't tackling running backs or slamming quarterbacks to the turf, he was bragging about his prowess on the field or spewing trash talk at opposing players. But Sapp was more than a lot of hot air. A track star in high school, Sapp was remarkably quick for such a large man. He was remarkably strong as well. In his 9 years with the team, he made 310 tackles and 77 sacks. Perhaps his favorite quarterback to bring down was Green Bay Packers star Brett Favre, who shared his competitive nature and playfully sparred with the talkative Buccaneers standout. Not everyone appreciated Sapp's outrageous comments and disruptive behavior, though. He was fined by the league more than once and was even ejected for unsportsmanlike behavior in 2007. Sapp, who played with the Oakland Raiders for four seasons after leaving the Bucs, retired from football in 2008.

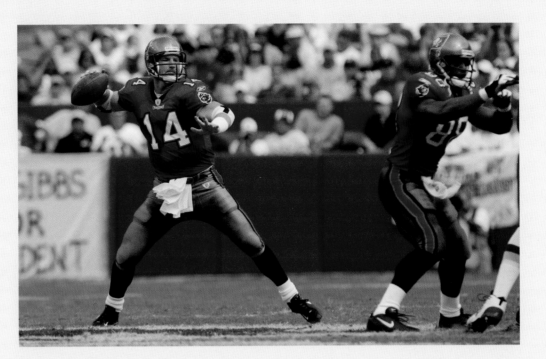

veteran quarterback Brad Johnson was added to the roster.
Unfortunately, both years, the Bucs met the red-hot Eagles
in wintry conditions at Philadelphia's Veterans Stadium in the
playoffs. Each time, the Eagles sank the Bucs.

After watching the Bucs stumble in the playoffs four
times in six seasons, team owner Malcolm Glazer and general
manager Rich McKay ran out of patience. And so, two days
after the 2001 season ended, McKay fired the immensely
popular Dungy. Both fans and players were shocked. "I'm at a
loss for words," said cornerback Ronde Barber. "He should be
remembered for how he pulled this franchise from the ashes.
He made it into something."

X Never known
for his arm strength,
Brad Johnson instead
directed the Buccaneers
offense with smart,
precise passing.

X Sometimes controversial and often boastful, Keyshawn Johnson backed up the talk by making a franchise-record 106 catches in 2001.

PUTTING THE
PIECES TOGETHER

Glazer replaced Dungy with Jon Gruden, who had been the

head coach of the Oakland Raiders. While Dungy had been

a quiet man known for his defensive prowess, Gruden was

a fiery coach with a background in offense, and he liked his

teams to put a lot of points on the board.

Before the 2002 season began, Gruden gathered his

offensive players inside Raymond James Stadium for a pep

talk. "See that pirate ship up there?" he asked, pointing to

the replica ship built into the stadium's stands. "See those

guys up there? They want to fire the cannons. If we don't

execute and get in the red zone [inside the 20-yard line], they

can't do their jobs. So let's put those guys to work and get in

the red zone, all right?"

The cannons did fire frequently at Raymond James

Stadium in 2002—the team scored almost 200 points in 8

home games—but still, it was the defense that Dungy had

built that saved the season. In five straight games, the

defense allowed just one touchdown; twice, the defense shut

out the opposing offense altogether. Relentless defensive

end Simeon Rice was among the stars, leading the NFC with

15.5 sacks and forcing 6 fumbles. In the final game of the

season, the Bucs beat the Bears in chilly Chicago, 15–0, on

five Gramatica field goals.

Tampa Bay's franchise-best 12–4 record was good enough to earn the team a first-round playoff bye before the Bucs hosted the 49ers in the second round. The Bucs rolled to an overwhelming 31–6 victory to reach the NFC Championship Game, which again took them to Philadelphia's Veterans Stadium. But Tampa Bay's season did not end there in 2002. Late in the fourth quarter, Barber intercepted a pass by Eagles quarterback Donovan McNabb and ran it back 92 yards to clinch a 27–10 victory and the team's first trip to the Super Bowl.

Super Bowl XXXVII pitted Gruden's Buccaneers against the Raiders, the team he had been coaching just a year earlier. Although the Raiders took an early 3–0 lead, the Tampa Bay defense quieted Oakland's high-powered offense the rest of the way. The Bucs set a Super Bowl record with five interceptions, three of which were returned for touchdowns, as Tampa Bay ran away to a 48–21 blowout. Dexter Jackson, the safety who had snagged two of those interceptions, was rewarded with the game's MVP trophy. "By God," Gruden yelled as he hoisted the Lombardi Trophy above his head. "This night belongs to Tampa Bay!"

Great things were expected of the Super Bowl champions in 2003, but the season turned out to be a letdown. First, injuries sidelined both Alstott and wide receiver Joe Jurevicius. Then,

COURTING A COACH

Jon Gruden (pictured) wasn't Tampa Bay's first choice. Buccaneers ownership had actually intended to hire longtime NFL coach Bill Parcells to replace Tony Dungy in 2002. When Parcells bowed out, the Bucs appeared ready to snatch coach Steve Mariucci away from the San Francisco 49ers. But then team owner Malcolm Glazer returned from a trip to California with Gruden in tow instead. Even as they were courting Mariucci, the Bucs had also been negotiating with Oakland Raiders owner Al Davis, who expected a lot in return for the young coach who had taken his team to a pair of divisional titles. The two sides finally settled on the terms of what was essentially a trade—Tampa Bay surrendered two first-round draft picks, two second-round draft picks, and $8 million in cash—before Davis called Gruden at 1:00 A.M. to inform him of the decision. By 5:30 A.M., Gruden had agreed to a 5-year, $17.5-million contract to coach the Buccaneers. A year later, at the age of 39, he became the youngest coach ever to win a Super Bowl.

RUNNING FOR THE RECORD

They had been trying for 32 years. But none of the 1,864 kickoffs that the Tampa Bay Buccaneers had received before December 16, 2007, had been returned for a touchdown. Then, on the 1,865th try, in a game against the Atlanta Falcons, a young receiver named Michael Spurlock burst through a hole in the middle of the field and sprinted 90 yards along the right sideline to reach the end zone untouched. Even as the play was unfolding, however, neither his coach nor his teammates were sure that one of the most dubious streaks in NFL history would actually be broken. Coach Jon Gruden later said that he assumed that Spurlock would step out of bounds or that a penalty would negate the return. But as the crowd at Tampa Bay's Raymond James Stadium roared and players jumped up and down on the sidelines, Spurlock crossed the goal line successfully. "[Linebacker] Derrick Brooks always tells me, 'Today is the day to make history,'" Spurlock said after the game. "And it happened. Everybody got their block, I hit it, and I found the end zone."

Keyshawn Johnson, who had been complaining about his role in the offense, was benched for the final four games of the season. By the end of the year, the team was a disappointing 7–9, below the .500 mark for the first time since 1996. Then, before the start of the 2004 campaign, both Sapp and Lynch left the team. With new players learning the ropes, the Bucs posted their second straight losing season.

But 2005 started out with a renewed sense of optimism in Tampa Bay. Exciting rookie running back Carnell "Cadillac" Williams rushed 1,178 yards, despite injuring his ankle. After winning the newly formed NFC South Division with an 11–5 record, the Buccaneers found themselves back in the playoffs. Unfortunately, the Redskins held Williams to just 49 yards, and young quarterback Chris Simms turned the ball over 3 times as Tampa Bay lost 17–10.

Injuries were the main story throughout 2006. The worst injury was that of Simms, who suffered a ruptured spleen early in the season. Although his replacement, Bruce Gradkowski, and receiver Joey Galloway played valiantly, the Buccaneers started the season 0–4 and ended with a 4–12 record that was the worst in the division.

That dramatic decline was halted when journeyman quarterback Jeff Garcia joined the team in 2007 and, with

Obtained in 2005, longtime Giants receiver Ike Hilliard was part of coach Jon Gruden's plan to build a new, high-powered offense in Tampa Bay.

TONY DUNGY

COACH
BUCCANEERS SEASONS: 1996-2001

Tony Dungy's name had been mentioned as a candidate for several NFL head coaching positions before he finally landed such a job. A former NFL defensive back who won a Super Bowl with the Pittsburgh Steelers in 1978, Dungy had been an assistant coach for 16 years before being offered the top job in Tampa Bay in 1996. Dungy quickly proved that he was perfect for the position. He introduced his "Cover 2" defensive plan, which relies on speed and agility to be successful, and in his second season with the team, the Buccaneers enjoyed their first winning season in 15 years. Dungy's team made four playoff appearances during his tenure in Tampa, advancing as far as the NFC Championship Game in 1999. Dungy was a soft-spoken man whose Christian upbringing influenced his coaching style; he was known as a patient teacher who tried not to berate or belittle his players. When he couldn't coax enough scoring from his team to reach the Super Bowl, however, he was fired after the 2001 season. In 2006, Dungy won a Super Bowl as coach of the Indianapolis Colts.

the help of young defensive tackle Donald Penn, turned the downward spiral around. "We're going to find a way to clinch this division," Garcia said as the Bucs neared the end of the season with a winning record. "We're going to go into the playoffs, and we're going to battle whoever we have to play."

Although Tampa Bay returned to prominence with a 9–7 record, first in the NFC South, Garcia and the Buccaneers had the misfortune of playing the surging New York Giants in the first round of the playoffs, and their season ended with a 24–14 loss to the eventual Super Bowl champions. In 2008, linebacker Barrett Ruud helped the Bucs streak to a 9–3 start, but they then lost their last four games—a painful collapse that left the team out of the playoffs and Gruden out of a job. The coach was fired and replaced by 32-year-old assistant coach Raheem Morris.

For the Tampa Bay Buccaneers and their fans, the journey from the worst start in NFL history to a Super Bowl championship was a long, rough road. But after investing so much time to get to the top, the Bucs are now ready to create their own legend in Tampa Bay. In a region with such a colorful past, the Tampa Bay Buccaneers hope to forge a golden future.

INDEX

Alstott, Mike 24, 28, 30, 40

Barber, Ronde 35, 40

Bell, Ricky 13, 27

Bennett, Leeman 16, 19

Brooks, Derrick 22, 23, 24, 42

Buccaneers name 9

Carrier, Mark 19

Culverhouse, Hugh 16

Davis, John 30

Dilfer, Trent 22, 24, 30

division championships 14, 43, 47

Dungy, Tony 22, 32, 35, 39, 41, 46

Dunn, Warrick 24

first season 10, 12

Galloway, Joey 43

Garcia, Jeff 43, 47

Glazer, Malcolm 35, 39, 41

Gradkowski, Bruce 43

Gramatica, Martin 30, 39

Green, Dave 10

Gruden, Jon 39, 40, 41, 42, 47

Husted, Michael 30

Jackson, Bo 19, 27

Jackson, Dexter 40

Johnson, Brad 35

Johnson, Keyshawn 32, 43

Jurevicius, Joe 40

King, Shaun 30

Lynch, John 22, 24, 30, 43

McKay, John 9, 10, 12, 16

McKay, Rich 35

Morris, Raheem 47

MVP award 40

NFC Championship Game 14, 32, 40, 46

NFL championships 40, 47

NFL records 10

Nickerson, Hardy 24

Pear, Dave 10

Penn, Donald 47

Perkins, Ray 19, 21

playoffs 14, 15, 16, 20, 24, 29, 30, 32, 35, 40, 43, 46, 47

Pro Bowl 23, 28

Pro Football Hall of Fame 11, 27

Raymond James Stadium 29, 31, 39, 42

retired numbers 11

Rhett, Errict 22

Rice, Simeon 39

Rudolph, Council 10

Ruud, Barrett 47

Sapp, Warren 22, 24, 34, 43

Selmon, Lee Roy 10, 11, 16, 27

Simms, Chris 43

Spurlock, Michael 42

Spurrier, Steve 10

Super Bowl 28, 40, 41, 47

Super Bowl records 40

Tampa Stadium 13, 24, 31

team records 24, 28, 30, 40

Testaverde, Vinny 19, 21, 22, 27

Thomas, Broderick 21

uniform change 20, 24

Wilder, James 14

Williams, Carnell "Cadillac" 43

Williams, Doug 13, 15, 16

Williamson, Richard 21

Wood, Richard 14

Wyche, Sam 21, 22

Young, Steve 19, 27